# I NEED TO
# LOVE GOD

# GOD AND ME

## BOOKS IN SERIES

I Need to Trust in God
I Need to Hope in God
I Need to Love God
I Need to Love Other People

# I NEED TO
# LOVE GOD

Joel and Mary Beeke

Illustrated by Cassandra Clark

Reformation Heritage Books
Grand Rapids, Michigan

*I Need to Love God*
© 2021 by Joel and Mary Beeke

**Reformation Heritage Books**
3070 29th St. SE
Grand Rapids, MI 49512
616-977-0889
orders@heritagebooks.org
www.heritagebooks.org

*Printed in China*
21 22 23 24 25 26/10 9 8 7 6 5 4 3 2 1

Library of Congress Cataloging-in-Publication Data

Names: Beeke, Joel R., 1952– author. | Beeke, Mary, author. | Clark, Cassandra, illustrator.
Title: I need to love God / Joel and Mary Beeke ; illustrated by Cassandra Clark.
Description: Grand Rapids, Michigan : Reformation Heritage Books, [2021] | Series: God and me | Audience: Ages 4–7
Identifiers: LCCN 2021002921 | ISBN 9781601788719 (hardcover)
Subjects: LCSH: God (Christianity)—Worship and love—Juvenile literature.
Classification: LCC BV4817 .B34 2021 | DDC 241/.4—dc23
LC record available at https://lccn.loc.gov/2021002921

*For additional Reformed literature, request a free book list from Reformation Heritage Books at the above regular or email address.*

## MEMORY VERSE

"We love him, because he first loved us" (1 John 4:19).

Sophie rushed into the house.
She flopped onto the chair.
"We won the game!"

"Mom, may I have a cookie please?"

"Sorry, Sophie, the cookies are for our neighbors."

"But I'm hungry!"

"We will have supper in a half hour."

"I want a cookie!
I need a cookie!"

"Sophie, go to your room. Come out when you are ready to say you're sorry."

"I was wrong, Mom. I'm sorry."

"I didn't respond to Mom like the commandment in the Bible says I should. And I got mad. Please forgive me."

"God created our amazing world and has blessed me so much!"

"How could I sin against a kind, loving, and holy God who is always better to me than I am to Him? I need to love God."

"Help me to love Thee, Lord Jesus, now and forever. Help me to love Thee more than I love anything else in this world—even more than I love Mom and Dad. For Jesus's sake. Amen."

# TALK ABOUT IT

1. How does the Holy Spirit teach us to love God more than anything or anyone else?

2. How will our lives change and show new obedience when we truly love God for saving us in Jesus Christ?

Note to parents: God commands us to love Him with all our heart, soul, and mind (Matt. 22:37). Explain to your children that they need the Holy Spirit to give them a heart to love and obey God, their parents, and their brothers and sisters. Such a love for God is always the fruit of saving faith (Gal. 5:6).